the Stories Behind the Music

Christmas Carol Devotions and Activities for Your Family

REVISED & EXPANDED

LUKE & TRISHA GILKERSON

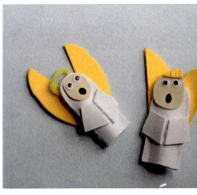

Other books by Luke and Trisha Gilkerson

Christ in the Commandments:
A Family Study of the Ten Commandments

•

Foes, Fiends, and Failures:
A Study of the Bad Guys of Pilgrim's Progress

•

Laying the Foundation:
A Family Study of the Apostles' Creed

•

Praying with Paul:
A Family Prayer Guide

•

The Heart of Humility:
A Family Study of Philippians 2:1-18

•

The Talk:
7 Lessons to Introduce Your Child to Biblical Sexuality

•

Losing It:
A Christian Parent's Guide to Overcoming Anger

Contents

Introduction

We've never had to teach our kids to like Christmas carols. We love to saturate our house with music throughout the year, but during the month of December, Christmas songs fill the atmosphere. While we're not much for Santa songs, we love the typical winter carols that dominate the radio in December. We love rockin' around the Christmas tree with Brenda Lee, learning what Christmas means to Stevie Wonder, and dreaming of a white Christmas with Bing Crosby.

But the carols that really grab our hearts are those that celebrate the true meaning of Christmas: the birth of Christ.

Several years ago we were visiting relatives around Thanksgiving and got to talking about what we wanted to do to really celebrate Jesus' birth at Christmas. We wanted to come up with something creative and memorable, and when we remembered how much our kids love Christmas songs, we thought perhaps we could use music to instruct them.

That's how this little book started. We took 15 of our favorite Christmas carols and wove them together to tell the story of the birth of the greatest Man who ever lived. We hope these simple devotions bless your family as well.

HOW TO USE THIS BOOK

Do just one lesson per day, whenever it feels most natural for your family.

For some families, Christmas Day is the culmination of a month of anticipation and celebration. For other families, Christmas is just the beginning of the Christmas season (originally called The Twelve Days of Christmas) leading up to Epiphany on January 6. Use the natural rhythms of the holiday season as your calendar for these devotionals.

You might choose to start 15 days before Christmas to time the last devotional for Christmas Eve. (You also might start earlier if you know the holidays will get hectic and you need to skip a day or two.) You could also start on Christmas Eve and read through the whole Christmas season, up through Epiphany.

1. **Gather Your Kids Together:** Find a cozy place together as a family. Pick a room in the house that is best decorated with Christmas cheer.

2. **Sing:** Do what best works for your family. Do you have CDs or playlists with these songs? Do you like to sing a cappella? Does someone in your family know how to play an accompanying instrument well? You might want to sing the song

together a couple times: once at the beginning of the lesson and once at the end. (Or, if you have kids like ours who turn into distracted singing monsters when music plays, you might want to save the singing until the end.) To get access to free playlists of all the songs in this book, go to IntoxicatedOnLife. com/carols.

3. **Tell the Story of the Carol:** Each carol comes with a story of how or why it was written. Each story is written to remind kids about our spiritual heritage, those in the church who have loved these songs for many generations.

4. **Read the Scripture:** Each song comes with an accompanying passage from the Bible. Read the passage aloud for your kids to hear or have one of your children read it aloud if they are old enough.

5. **Explain the Scripture:** Each lesson comes with a short written explanation of what the Scripture means. The lessons are written interactively to encourage your kids to think out loud about what the Bible is saying.

6. **Discuss the Scripture:** Each lesson comes with a few simple comprehension and application questions to help your children think more deeply about the gospel.

7. **Pray:** Each lesson ends with a simple prayer related to the reading.

8. **Sing Again:** Encourage your kids to sing their hearts out! Give them space to dance or move around if they want.

9. **Crafts:** Each lesson has a corresponding craft. You may choose to do some or all of the crafts. Be sure to read the instructions ahead of time so you know how much time you'll need and how to prepare.

A NOTE ABOUT THE CRAFTS

I'm not a super-crafty mom. I don't sit down and do fun crafts with my kids on a daily, weekly, or even monthly basis. I have kids that *love* crafts, though! Even I do. I think most of us do. What's the problem then?

The problem for me is crafts are just not a priority. I get busy with the day to day rush. Doing the laundry. Finishing school work. Making meals. Working from home. Family devotions. There's so much to do in our every day life that crafts just don't make the cut. What I've found, though, is if I take the time to slow down in certain seasons, it can have a beautiful impact on my family.

Let me encourage you to slow down. Slow down just for a couple of weeks during the Christmas season. I know this season of shopping, baking, planning, decorating, and parties can be one of the busiest, but if we want to intentionally take time to focus on Christ with our families, we have to learn to say "no" to some things. Even good things. We say "no" to good things so we can say "yes" to the best things.

Take the time to work through each of the devotions and at least a few (or all) of the crafts that most interest your family. The crafts are a great way to make the devotions more memorable to your family. You'll be able to look at the ornament or wall hanging you made next year and remember what you learned from the Christmas carol you studied. Crafts are a great way to build family memories. Your children will cherish the memories they have of you sitting together around the table working on a creative project. The creative play that comes from these projects will help to even further engage the minds of your family to meditate upon the truth's of Scripture.

We'd invite you to stop by our Facebook page (facebook.com/intoxicatedonlife) and share pictures of the crafts your family has completed! It would delight us to see what you're doing together as a family.

Praying for the sweetest blessings from our Savior to your family this Christmas season.

Blessings,

Trisha

O Come, O Come, Emmanuel

STORY:

Over a thousand years ago, churches had special times of celebration every night the week before Christmas. What a fun way to build up to Christmas day! People would gather into church buildings and listen to two choirs, seated at opposite ends of the room. These choirs would sing back and forth to each other. Every night they sang a different song, and every night the songs were filled with prophecies from the Old Testament about Christ.

Did you know that hundreds of years before Jesus was born, God sent prophets to foretell about His coming? Have you heard of any prophecies in the Bible that predicted Christ coming? (*See if your child can remember any.*) The prophets foretold *where* He would be born, *when* He would be born, the family He would be born into, how He would minister to people, His death on the cross, and His resurrection from the dead. There were literally hundreds of details the prophets told us about Jesus long before He came.

About 800 years ago, someone in the church took some of these prophecies and put them together into a song to celebrate the Christmas season. It is the song we know today as "O Come, O Come Emmanuel." This song is all about the prophecies God gave to us about Christ before He came.

SCRIPTURE: MATTHEW 1:18-23

EXPLANATION:

Joseph and Mary were supposed to get married. Do you know any one who is engaged or who just got married? (*See if your child can name anyone.*) But Mary was already pregnant with a baby. An angel came to Joseph in a dream to tell him that the one who was in Mary's womb was a special child. He said the child should be named "Jesus," because Jesus' name means "the Lord saves."

What would Jesus save people from? (*Their sins.*) The penalty for sin is death: it is what we deserve for disobeying God. Everyone is guilty, and without God's forgiveness, all of us would die and be separated from God forever. But as the song says, Jesus came to give us victory over the grave. If we believe in Christ, we will live forever with Him in a world without sin or death. What do you think eternity with God will be like? (*See what your child says about this.*)

The reason Jesus could save us from our sin is because he was not just any human child. He is God. One of His names in the Bible is Emmanuel, which means "God with us." We can celebrate what the song promises: 2000 years ago, Emmanuel came to us, and some day in the future He'll come back to us again. God's desire is to be with us forever, just as the name *Emmanuel* tells us. One of the last promises written in the Bible tells us that one day God will transform this whole world: "Behold, the dwelling place of God is with man. He will dwell with them, and they will be his people, and God himself will be with them as their God" (Revelation 21:3).

QUESTIONS FOR YOUR KIDS:

1. Can you remember: what does the name Emmanuel mean? (*God with us.*)

2. What does that mean that Jesus is called Emmanuel? (*Jesus is God in human flesh, and he came to live with us on Earth.*)

3. Why do you think God gave His people prophecies about the coming of Christ? (*First, He did this so we could have hope that God would save us from our sins. Second, He did it so we would recognize the Savior when He came to Earth.*)

PRAY:

We rejoice, Jesus, because you are Emmanuel, God with us. Thank you for coming to be with us. We look forward to the day when you will come again and change this whole world, and we will be with you forever.

EMMANUEL DOVE

Doves are seen all throughout the Bible as symbols of peace and the presence of the Holy Spirit. In the New Testament, they are present at scenes associated with Jesus' infancy, baptism, and in the week of his death. This simple dove craft will keep little hands busy making lovely decorations for your home. With the addition of some fishing line and tape, you can create a festive environment by hanging these from the ceiling.

SUPPLIES:

- Paper plate
- Coffee filters
- Red craft foam
- Yellow craft foam
- Googly eyes
- Glitter
- Craft glue

DIRECTIONS:

1. Fold a paper plate in half, pressing in a sharp crease so the plate will stand up when folded.

2. Fold coffee filters in half and glue to each side of the plate to make the dove's wings.

3. Use craft glue to spell out the word "Emmanuel" on a piece of red craft foam. If a younger child is doing this you may wish to write it in pencil first so they can trace it with the glue.

4. Sprinkle glitter generously on the glue and allow to dry.

5. Cut out the word "Emmanuel" from the red foam making a wavy banner shape. Glue the banner to the side of your dove.

6. Using yellow foam, cut 2 triangles the same size and glue them to either side of the plate at the front corner. This is the dove's beak. Add googly eyes on both sides behind the beak.

7. Display the dove on a shelf, table, mantle, or add a string to the top and hang it.

O Come, O Come, Emmanuel

12th Century Latin, tr. John Mason Neale

15th Century French melody, arr Thomas Helmore

1. O come, O come, Em - man - u - el, And ran - som cap - tive Is - ra - el, That
2. O come, Thou Wis - dom from on high, Who or - derest all things might - i - ly; To
3. O come, Thou Rod of Jes - se, free Thine own from Sa - tan's tyr - an - ny; From
4. O come, Thou Day - spring, come and cheer Our spir - its by Thine ad - vent here; Dis-
5. O come, Thou Key of Da - vid, come, And op - en wide our heav - enly home; Make
6. O come, O come, great Lord of might, Who to Thy tribes on Si - nai's height In
7. O come, Thou Root of Jes - se's tree, An en - sign of Thy peo - ple be; Be-
8. O come, De - sire of na - tions, bind In one the hearts of all man - kind; Bid

mourns in lone - ly ex - ile here Un - til the Son of God ap - pear.
us the path of know - ledge show, And teach us in her ways to go.
depths of hell Thy peo - ple save, And give them vic - tory over the grave.
- perse the gloom - y clouds of night, And death's dark sha - dows put to flight.
safe the way that leads on high, And close the path to mis - er - y. Re-
an - cient times once gave the law In cloud and ma - jes - ty and awe.
- fore Thee rul - ers si - lent fall; All peo - ples on Thy mer - cy call.
Thou our sad di - vi - sions cease, And be Thy - self our King of Peace.

Refrain

- joice! Re - joice! Em - man - u - el shall come to thee, O Is - ra - el.

O Little Town of Bethlehem

STORY:

About a century and a half ago, Philip Brooks was a preacher who lived in Philadelphia, Pennsylvania. In 1865 he took a trip to Israel to see the lands where Jesus walked. Do you think it would be fun to visit Israel? (*See if there are any places in Israel your child would want to see.*) On Christmas Eve, Brooks and his companions traveled on horseback from Jerusalem to Bethlehem, the town where Jesus was born. After a two-hour trip they came to a field where, tradition says, shepherds saw the angels filling the sky, announcing the Savior's birth.

That night he participated in a worship service at a 1,400-year-old church building called the Church of the Nativity, which was built over a cave believed to be the birthplace of Jesus. Philip Brooks writes, "I remember standing in the old church in Bethlehem, close to the spot where Jesus was born, when the whole church was ringing hour after hour with splendid hymns of praise to God, how again and again it seemed as if I could hear voices I knew well, telling each other of the wonderful night of the Savior's birth."

Three years later Brooks wrote "O Little Town of Bethlehem" for the children's choir at his church. Having seen the town of Bethlehem with his own eyes, he was amazed that someone so wonderful could have been born in such a small, insignificant place.

SCRIPTURE: LUKE 2:4-6

EXPLANATION:

A thousand years before Jesus came along, Bethlehem was the birthplace of King David, which gave it the nickname "the city of David." It was a really small town. Later the prophet Micah said even though Bethlehem was a very insignificant place, it would be the place the next great ruler of Israel would come from—the Messiah.

Joseph and Mary made their way to Bethlehem, not because they really wanted to go, but because the government told them they must go. Both Joseph and Mary were King David's descendants, and God was going to make sure that Jesus the Messiah was born in the city of David, in Bethlehem.

Jesus wasn't born in a big important city. Can you think of any really big, important cities in the world today? (*See if your child can think of any big cities.*)

Instead, Jesus was born in the little town of Bethlehem. Jesus wasn't born during the hustle and bustle of the daytime, but at night when most people were sleeping. Jesus was the great King, but he wasn't born in the royal city of Jerusalem where prophets and priests could announce his birth to the world. He was born where hardly anyone would notice him. If you had been resting in Bethlehem that night, chances are you might not have noticed anything different about the night.

When Jesus grew up, He said this is how the kingdom of God comes into the world for now. Some day, Jesus will return with a trumpet blast for all to hear, but for now, Jesus said, "The kingdom of God is not coming in ways that can be observed, nor will they say, 'Look, here it is!' or 'There!' for behold, the kingdom of God is in the midst of you" (Luke 17:20-21). God's kingdom is still in the midst of us right now, even when we can't see it.

QUESTIONS FOR YOUR KIDS:

1. Can you remember: what town was Jesus born in? (*Bethlehem.*)

2. Why was Jesus born in such a hidden, out-of-the-way place? (*God was showing the humility of Jesus. He wasn't born in a big, important place but in a small town. God isn't only working when he does big, exciting miracles. He's also at work in small, unnoticeable ways.*)

PRAY:

Thank you, God, for fulfilling your promise to make Jesus born in the city of King David. It is one of the reasons we know Jesus is our King. Thank you for being at work in our lives in ways we don't even know. Even if the world ignores You, God, we are so excited You are involved in every detail of our lives.

BETHLEHEM ORNAMENT

While considering the carol "O Little Town of Bethlehem," I pictured the roads Mary and Joseph walked down and the buildings they passed in their quest for a room. This simple ornament shows a silhouette of the silent, small town of Bethlehem and the star that illuminated the night sky. Pull it out every year to decorate your tree, and let it serve as a reminder of both this time with your family and the Holy Family long ago.

SUPPLIES:

- Clear, round plastic ornaments
- Fine gold glitter
- Craft glue
- Blue and black craft paint
- Back permanent marker
- Small paint brushes
- Polyurethane spray (optional)

DIRECTIONS:

1. Remove the top hanging part of your ornament and set aside for later.

2. Pour a small amount of blue craft paint inside the ornament and shake well. Add more paint as needed to completely coat the inside.

3. Place ornament upside down in a small paper cup and allow excess paint to drip out for several hours.

4. To create the silhouette of the buildings, freehand the outline with a black permanent marker. Rounded rooftops, small windows, and a few palm trees are fairly easy to recreate. You're not going for perfection here, just the general idea.

5. Give your child a small paint brush and black paint to fill in the buildings.

6. Set the ornament back on the cup and let the paint fully dry.

7. Draw a star in the sky and fill in the windows using glue then sprinkle with glitter. Tap the ornament gently to knock off excess glitter.

8. Let the ornament dry completely. If you desire to extend the life and durability of the ornament add a coat of clear spray.

O Little Town of Bethlehem

Phillips Brooks, 1867   Lewis Henry Redner

1. O lit-tle town of Bethle-hem, how still we see thee lie! A-bove thy deep and dream-less sleep the si-lent stars go by. Yet in thy dark streets shin-eth the ev-er-last-ing Light; The hopes and fears of all the years are met in thee to-night.

2. For Christ is born of Ma-ry, and ga-thered all a-bove, While mor-tals sleep, the an-gels keep their watch of won-dering love. O morn-ing stars to-ge-ther, pro-claim the ho-ly birth, And prais-es sing to God the King, and peace to men on earth!

3. How si-lent-ly, how silent-ly, the won-drous Gift is giv'n; So God im-parts to hu-man hearts the bless-ings of His heav'n. No ear may hear His com-ing, but in this world of sin, Where meek souls will re-ceive Him still, the dear Christ en-ters in.

4. Where child-ren pure and hap-py pray to the bless-èd Child, Where mis-er-y cries out to Thee, Son of the mo-ther mild; Where char-i-ty stands watch-ing and faith holds wide the door, The dark night wakes, the glor-y breaks, and Christ-mas comes once more.

5. O ho-ly Child of Bethle-hem, de-scend to us, we pray; Cast out our sin, and en-ter in, be born in us to-day. We hear the Christ-mas an-gels the great glad tid-ings tell; O come to us, a-bide with us, our Lord Em-man-u-el!

Away in a Manger

STORY:

The song "Away in a Manger" first appeared about 130 years ago in a book called *The Little Children's Book for Schools and Families*. It was called "Luther's Cradle Hymn," and it was probably written in honor of the famous church leader Martin Luther on the 400th anniversary of his birth.

The song speaks of the manger Christ was placed in after he was born. Do you know what a manger is? (*A manger is food trough for animals, made of either wood or metal or stone.*) The Bible doesn't mention if any animals were around Jesus when he was born, but since there was a manger, there probably were some animals there. It's amazing to think that there was no comfortable crib waiting for Jesus when he was born—only a dirty manger used for feeding animals.

Because the song was written like a lullaby, it is a very popular song today for children's choirs.

SCRIPTURE: LUKE 2:7

EXPLANATION:

When they came to Bethlehem, Mary and Joseph didn't find lodging in a nice hotel. No one had room for them, not even their distant relatives that lived there. Instead, they found housing in a nearby cave or shelter for animals. When Mary gave birth to Jesus, she wasn't in a nice room, surrounded by family or friends or even a doctor to help her. Joseph was the only one there.

Mary didn't have a nursery to put her new baby in—not even a crib. She had to lay him in a feeding trough called a manger. Imagine little Jesus waking up to the sound of cows mooing the way the song says. Animals would make strange roommates on the first night of your life. Which would be the weirdest farm animal to have in your room? (*See what your child says.*)

Jesus was born into very humble conditions. He was born into a poor family, suffered the same way we all suffer, and would live most of his life in small towns surrounded by poor, simple people. Jesus did not come into the world to be served by others like a king, but to serve and love others.

QUESTIONS FOR YOUR KIDS:

1. Can you remember: what was Jesus laid inside after he was born? (*A manger, which was a feeding trough for animals.*)

2. Was Jesus born into a rich family or a poorer family? (*A poorer family.*)

3. Why wasn't Jesus born in a rich family, surrounded by wealth and comfort? (*Jesus came to Earth to experience the suffering caused by human sin. One of the ways he suffered is by experiencing the suffering of poverty.*)

PRAY:

Thank You, God, for sending Jesus to live a humble life. For our sakes Jesus became poor so that we could become spiritually rich. Make us humble like Jesus Christ, looking not just to our own interests, but also to the interests of others.

PEG DOLL NATIVITY FAMILY

"Away in a Manger" has always been one of my favorites. Even as a child, I could sense the reverence of the words and the importance of the tiny baby Jesus—God coming to earth, born in a manger with no crib of his own. We have several nativity scenes we put out each year, including a plastic one our kids have had since they were young. They love being able to play with the nativity figurines. We decided to make our own version and had a lot of fun painting this little keepsake as we studied the song.

SUPPLIES

- Unfinished peg doll family set
- Craft Paint
- Mini craft sticks
- Rafia or hay pieces
- White fabric scraps
- Small paintbrushes
- Paint pens (optional)
- Painters tape (optional)

DIRECTIONS:

1. Paint the clothes on the body. If you have smaller children, tape off the head with painter's tape so it stays clean while painting. Once the base clothes are painted, set your dolls aside to dry for about an hour.

2. Paint head coverings, details on the clothes, and add the face. A fine paint pen is best for adding these small details. All you need to paint of the baby Jesus is hair and face details.

3. Wrap baby Jesus with white scrap, leaving just his face and part of his head showing.

4. While the remaining paint is drying you can build the manger to hold Jesus. Make an x with two mini craft sticks, secure in center with hot glue. Repeat with another 2 sticks. These will be the leg supports to your manger.

5. Run a length of hot glue down the inner edge of one of the X's, press 3 mini craft sticks into glue. Repeat at the other end, placing your second X to secure your manger, and then glue 3 more sticks to the other side.

Away in a Manger

Anonymous, 1885

James Ramsey Murray, 1887

1. A - way in a man-ger, no crib for a bed, The lit - tle Lord Je - sus laid
2. The cat - tle are low - ing, the Ba - by a - wakes, But lit - tle Lord Je - sus, no
3. Be near me, Lord Je - sus, I ask Thee to stay Close by me for - ev - er, and

down His sweet head. The stars in the sk - y looked down where He lay, The
cry - ing He makes; I love Thee, Lord Je - sus, look down from the sky And
love me, I pray; Bless all the dear child-ren in Thy ten - der care, And

lit - tle Lord Je - sus, a - sleep on the hay.
stay by my cra - dle til morn-ing is nigh.
fit us for heav-en to live with Thee there.

Go, Tell It On the Mountain

STORY:

Slavery was legal in America until 1865. Before that, black Africans and others were regularly shipped to the United States and forced into a life of slavery. Many had no freedoms at all. Do you think it would be a difficult life as a slave? (*See how your child feels about that.*)

Black slaves were known for their music, which had a sound all of its own. Many times they didn't have instruments, so they had to use only their voices, hand clapping, and foot stomping. Some songs were sung while the slaves worked, making it easier to pass the day away when the work got hard. Some songs were for fun. Other songs were about God: they were called spirituals.

One of these spirituals from the days of slave life is "Go, Tell It on the Mountain." Most spirituals were never written down. They were passed on orally from plantation to plantation. So in the early 1900s a music professor named John Works did a lot of research and compiled a bunch of spirituals into a book, and "Go, Tell It on the Mountain" was one of them. Adding some words of his own, he preserved the tune so others could sing it. Thanks to his research, this Christmas tune was not lost but lives on in churches all around the world.

SCRIPTURE: LUKE 2:8-9

EXPLANATION:

The shepherds in Bethlehem were no ordinary shepherds. All the animals raised close to the city of Jerusalem—which was only six miles away—were designated as temple sacrifices. These were animals that were raised to be sacrificed in the temple some day. What would that feel like to raise little lambs knowing some day they would be sacrificed on an altar for people's sins? (*See how your child feels about a sweet little lamb being killed. This gives us a small taste of the awful price that must be paid for sin.*)

There was a special watchtower for shepherds on the outskirts of Bethlehem called the "tower for the flock." A lot of the Jews believed, based on their reading of the Old Testament, that when the Messiah arrived, God would announce it first from this special tower. Maybe these were the shepherds that worked near this tower.

The shepherds in Bethlehem were surprised that night. While they were watching their flock of sheep, an angel suddenly appeared and the bright light of God's glory shown around them. The Bible says they were filled with great fear.

Their job had been to raise lambs to be sacrificed in the temple. But God gave them a more important job: to go and see the true Lamb of God who would take away the sins of the whole world.

QUESTIONS FOR YOUR KIDS:

1. Can you remember: who were the first people told about Jesus birth? (*Shepherds.*)

2. What important job did these shepherds do? (*Raising lambs that would later be sacrificed for people's sins.*)

3. In the song, "Go, Tell It On the Mountain", it says we should be excited to tell people that God sent us salvation the day Jesus was born. What does that mean? (*Jesus came to take away our sins by dying on the cross. This is why the Bible calls Him the Lamb of God: He would be sacrificed on the cross to pay the penalty for our sins.*)

PRAY:

Thank You, God, that Jesus is the Savior of the world, that He came to die for us so we don't have to pay the eternal price for our sins. Give us the same attitude the shepherds had that night: to be in awe of You and to be excited about spreading the word about Jesus.

MOUNTAIN CANVAS

This "Go, Tell it on The Mountain" painting will be a fun, meaningful, addition to your holiday decorating. It looks lovely and is super simple to make—even for kids. We took advantage of painter's tape to help us define the sky from the mountains so even a shaky hand can paint it beautifully. With just a few art supplies, your family can create a keepsake that will become part of your decor year after year. The simplicity of this art coupled with the message of our Savior also makes a great statement year-round.

SUPPLIES:

- 11x14 Canvas
- Blue acrylic paint
- Green acrylic paint
- Black paint pen
- White paint pen
- Gold paint pen
- Painters tape
- Paintbrushes
- Pencil

DIRECTIONS:

1. Tape off a the shape of mountains with 2-3 peaks using painters tape. Wrap the tape around the sides of the canvas. Press the tape firmly into the canvas so you get a crisp paint line.

2. Begin by painting the sky first. Your brush strokes should start at the painters tape, brushing from the tape onto the canvas. Don't forget to paint the sides of your canvas. Allow to dry, and paint another coat if desired.

3. After the sky is dry, remove painters tape and re-tape where the sky meets the mountains. Again, press tape down firmly to get a sharp line. Paint each mountain using different brush strokes, which creates the illusion of depth. Don't forget to paint the sides of your canvas. Allow paint to dry completely. Paint a second coat if desired.

4. Once all your paint is dry, take a pencil and draw a Star of Bethlehem and your lyrics along the mountains. Trace over the words and star with a fine tipped paint pen. Allow your paint to dry. Erase any visible pencil marks.

Go, Tell It on the Mountain

African-American Spiritual

John Wesley Work, Jr., 1907

Angels from the Realms of Glory

STORY:

James Montgomery was born in Scotland, the son of a Moravian minister. His parents left on a mission trip to the island of Barbados in the Caribbean, leaving him at boarding school at the age of 5. Sadly, he never saw them again. When he was still young, his parents both died within a year of each other, leaving him orphaned.

As a boy, he didn't excel in school—flunking out at the age of 14. As a young man, he he tried many different jobs but they didn't work out. He tried being an apprentice to a baker, but hated the work. He moved to London to be a writer, but that also ended in failure. He moved from job to job, often being homeless for weeks at a time.

Finally, he became an assistant at a political newspaper, where he developed his skill and love of writing. He eventually became the owner of the newspaper and worked there for more than 30 years. There he was able to pursue his passions. He used the paper to publish his poetry. He wrote about spreading the gospel in foreign nations. He even spoke out against slavery and the causes of poverty.

One December, after reading the Gospel of Luke's account of Jesus' birth, he felt inspired to write a poem, and on Christmas Eve, 1816, he published the words in his newspaper to "Angels from the Realms of Glory." God proclaims the birth of Jesus to all people, rich and poor, Irish and English.

Years after Montgomery's death, the words of his song were set to new music and now this song is sung in English speaking churches all over the world.

SCRIPTURE: LUKE 2:10-12

EXPLANATION:

The angel's first words to the shepherds were to explain to them they were about to hear news of great joy and gladness. God had done something that night that should be cause for joy and celebration to the whole world: the Savior, the Messiah, had been born.

Notice the message is for all people—not just the shepherds in the field that night, not just the people in Bethlehem, not just the Jewish people. Everybody. For James Montgomery this was a powerful thought. The message of Christ's birth is for all the earth to know. Jesus is the Desire to Nations—all the nations of the world, not just the ones that know the gospel already. Jesus is a Savior for all types of people—rich and poor, slave and free. Everyone is in need of salvation.

The last stanza of the original song reminds us that we are all "doom'd for guilt to endless pains." We are all guilty before God. But because the Savior has come, our punishment can be revoked and we can be set free from sin. This is what we celebrate at Christmas and why the angels from the realms of glory were so full of praise that first Christmas night.

QUESTIONS FOR YOUR KIDS:

1. Why did the angels tell the shepherds not to be afraid? (*Because seeing an angel would cause anyone to be afraid. But the angels didn't come to punish or hurt anyone, but to give an announcement of joy.*)

2. Who did the angels say was born in the city of David? (*A Savior, Christ the Lord.*)

3. How is Jesus a Savior? (*He saves us from our sins. Because of Him we can be forgiven and be set free from sin.*)

PRAY:

Lord, fill us with joy over the coming of Jesus our Savior. He is your gift to the whole world. Give us love in our hearts for every person, knowing that you want all kinds of people all over the world to hear the message about Christ.

ANGEL SNOW "GLOBE"

One of my favorite Christmas crafts as a child was making a homemade snow globe. They're fun to make, you can upcycle an old jar you already have on hand, and they add a fun touch of whimsy to your Christmas decorations. For this one, we selected an inexpensive angel ornament and a sauce jar that I cleaned out and de-labeled. If you're feeling super-crafty, get out that big, old pickle jar you've been saving under the kitchen sink. This craft works with jars of all sizes.

SUPPLIES:

- Clean, smooth sided jar with lid
- Angel ornament
- Silver or white glitter
- Water
- Waterproof glue

DIRECTIONS:

1. Make sure that your ornament will fit inside your jar. A wide mouth jar will give you the most options.

2. Remove the hanger from the angel ornament top. Apply a generous amount of waterproof glue to the base of the angel ornament. Press it down firmly into the lid of the jar. Allow glue to cure and set according to package directions.

3. Pour glitter into the bottom of the jar, approximately a teaspoon to a teaspoon and a half.

4. Fill the jar with water leaving about a quarter to ⅛ of an inch space to make room for the ornament.

5. Apply glue to the inner ring and screw lid on tight. Turn the snow globe upright and enjoy!

Angels from the Realms of Glory

James Montgomery, 1816

Henry Thomas Smart, 1867

1. An - gels from the realms of glor-y, Wing your flight o'er all the earth;
2. Shep - herds, in the field a - bid - ing, Watch - ing o'er your flocks by night,
3. Sag - es, leave your con - tem-pla - tions, Bright - er vi - sions beam a - far;
4. Saints, be - fore the al - tar bend-ing, Watch - ing long in hope and fear;
5. Sin - ners, wrung with true re - pent-ance, Doomed for guilt to end - less pains,
6. Though an In - fant now we view Him, He shall fill His Fa - ther's throne,
7. All cre - a - tion, join in prais-ing God, the Fa - ther, Spir - it, Son,

Ye who sang cre - a - tion's stor - y Now pro - claim Mes - si - ah's birth.
God with us is now re - sid - ing; Yon - der shines the in - fant light:
Seek the great De - sire of na - tions; Ye have seen His na - tal star.
Sud - den - ly the Lord, de - scend-ing, In His tem - ple shall ap - pear.
Jus - tice now re - vokes the sent - ence, Mer - cy calls you, break your chains.
Ga - ther all the na - tions to Him; Eve - ry knee shall then bow down.
Ev - er - more your voic - es rais - ing To th'e - ter - nal Three in One.

Refrain

Come and wor-ship, come and wor-ship, Wor-ship Christ, the new-born king.

Hark! the Herald Angels Sing

STORY:

Charles Wesley wrote more than 6,000 hymns and songs for the church—6,000! If you wrote one song every day, it would take you more than 16 years to write 6,000 songs.

He wrote the song "Hark! The Herald Angels Sing" over 270 years ago and it is now one of his most famous songs. The words of the first line we know today are, "Hark! The herald angels sing, 'Glory to the newborn king.'" But those aren't the original words Wesley wrote. He wrote, "Hark, how all the welkin rings, 'Glory to the king of kings.'" What do you think a "welkin" is? (*See if your child can guess the meaning.*) The word "welkin" is an old word meaning heaven, where the angels live. So Wesley's first line is telling us to listen to the angels who live in the heavens glorifying the King of Kings, Jesus Christ.

It hasn't always had the tune we know today. Wesley's original tune for the song was the same as his song "Christ the Lord is Risen Today." Do you remember that song? (*See if your child can remember how that song goes.*) It wasn't until 100 years after the song was first published that the tune we now know was added to Wesley's lyrics.

SCRIPTURE: LUKE 2:13-14

EXPLANATION:

It wasn't just one angel that showed up in front of the shepherds. The Bible says that after the first angel spoke, suddenly a multitude of angels appeared. We don't know how many there were, but there could have been hundreds or even thousands.

Like the song says, these were "herald" angels. What's a herald? (*A herald is someone that proclaims or announces good news in a loud voice*). The song also says they were *singing*, but the Bible doesn't tell us that exactly. The Bible only tells us what they said that night: "Glory to God in the highest." This means that from the lowest creatures on earth to the very highest heavens, everyone should be praising God.

Then the angels said there would be peace on Earth among God's people. In that day, Jesus' family lived in the Roman Empire, and their emperor promised peace to all his citizens. But the way he bought peace was through his big army that forced people to obey him. But God's kingdom is different: it brings peace on Earth not by force, but by giving us peace with God. You see, because we're sinners, we want to be our own lord, our own boss—it's like we're at war with God. But when Jesus changes us on the inside, we start to call God our Lord, and God gives us the desire to please Him. God changes us from the inside out so we want to obey Him out of love. That's one of the reasons why the angels were so excited about the newborn king, Jesus: because He would give us peace with God.

QUESTIONS FOR YOUR KIDS:

1. Can you remember: the angels proclaimed that because Jesus was born, he would bring what on Earth? (*Peace.*)

2. How does God give us peace? (*He give us peace with Him, first. Just like the song says, "God and sinners reconciled." We are forgiven for all our sins and we are changed on the inside so that we want to obey God.*)

PRAY:

Thank You, God, for the birth of Jesus. We echo the same praise the angels gave that day so long ago: "Glory to God in the highest." We look forward to the day when there really will be peace all over the Earth, when the world is filled with Your worshipers.

FINGER PUPPET ANGELS

This classic Christmas carol centers around the angels singing a joyful song announcing the birth of the Savior! Your child can use this as a finger puppet as intended or they can be used as play figurines. Simply slip something like a large marker cap or a similar sized item inside and the puppets will stand up for play.

SUPPLIES:

- White craft foam
- Yellow craft foam
- Cream/tan craft foam
- White or yellow chenille stem
- Googly eyes
- Black permanent marker
- Hot glue gun
- Scissors

DIRECTIONS:

1. Cut 2 pieces of white craft foam into a finger shape (approx. 2" wide and 3" tall).

2. Cut a small circular piece for the face from the tan colored foam.

3. Cut wing pieces from the yellow craft foam: cut an oblong shape with a point on one end and a flat bottom; then cut it in half so the wings are symmetrical.

4. Run a generous bead of hot glue all along the edge of 1 piece of cut white foam.

5. Press the second piece of white craft foam onto the first, pressing firmly into the glue. Allow it to set for 2-3 minutes. Using craft glue will extend the drying time but it's recommended you use hot glue to secure the main body as it will hold the best.

6. Secure the face to the front and the wings to the back with glue.

7. Add a singing mouth to your angels using the black permanent marker.

8. Add an oversized piece of yellow craft foam to the back of the angels head for the hair and then trim the hair to the desired shape after gluing it on.

9. To make your angel's halo, cut a 1-inch piece of chenille stem or pipe cleaner. Bend it into a circle and glue to the back of the head.

10. Secure googly eyes to the face to finish.

Hark! The Herald Angels Sing

Charles Wesley, 1739

Felix Mendelssohn, 1840

1. Hark! The her-ald an-gels sing, "Glor-y to the new-born King; Peace on earth, and
2. Christ, by high-est heav'n a-dored; Christ the ev-er-last-ing Lord; Late in time, be-
3. Hail the heav'n-ly Prince of Peace! Hail the Sun of Right-eous-ness! Light and life to
4. Come, De-sire of na-tions, come, Fix in us Thy hum-ble home; Rise, the wo-man's
5. Ad-am's like-ness, Lord, ef-face, Stamp Thine im-age in its place: Se-cond Ad-am

mer-cy mild, God and sin-ners re-con-ciled!" Joy-ful, all ye na-tions rise,
-hold Him come, Off-spring of a vir-gin's womb. Veiled in flesh the God-head see;
all He brings, Ris'n with heal-ing in His wings. Mild He lays His glor-y by,
con-qu'ring Seed, Bruise in us the ser-pent's head. Now dis-play Thy sav-ing power,
from a-bove, Re-in-state us in Thy love. Let us Thee, though lost, re-gain,

Join the tri-umph of the skies; With th'an-gel-ic host pro-claim, "Christ is born in
Hail th'in-car-nate De-i-ty, Pleased with us in flesh to dwell, Je-sus our Em-
Born that man no more may die. Born to raise the sons of earth, Born to give them
Ru-ined na-ture now re-store; Now in mys-tic un-ion join Thine to ours, and
Thee, the Life, the in-ner man: O, to all Thy-self im-part, Formed in each be-

Refrain

Beth-le-hem!"
-man-u-el.
sec-ond birth. Hark! the her-ald an-gels sing, "Glor-y to the new-born King!"
ours to Thine.
-liev-ing heart.

O Come, All Ye Faithful

STORY:

The song, "O Come, All Ye Faithful", was not originally written in English but Latin. It was called "Adeste fideles." The author of the song, John Francis Wade, was a Roman Catholic music teacher who lived in England and later in France.

Wade was an artist in many ways. He hand-copied music sheets for churches and chapels to use all over Europe and America. He was a calligrapher, which means he could write in a very decorative handwriting style. He also wrote illuminated manuscripts, which means his books were decorated with beautiful borders and small illustrations on each page. He made his living teaching church music and Latin and by selling his manuscripts and chant books to choir leaders, schools, and wealthy families.

"O Come, All Ye Faithful" was sometimes called "The Portuguese Hymn" because in late 1700s, the song was performed in the chapel of the Portuguese embassy in London. When the Duke of Leeds heard it, he loved the triumphant lyrics and tune so much he commissioned a full arrangement of the song. The Duke conducted the song with a group of concert singers with the King's Concerts in London, which made the song popular throughout the whole country. Since then, it has been translated in more than 100 languages including the popular English version we know today.

SCRIPTURE: LUKE 2:15

EXPLANATION:

Here we see the immediate reaction of the shepherds after seeing the angels. They say to each other, "Let's go over to Bethlehem." They wanted to see the child the angels had spoken about.

That's what the song, "O Come, All Ye Faithful", invites us to do. It tells all faithful Christians to go to Bethlehem to adore Christ the Lord. Obviously, we can't go back in time and do what the shepherds did. But we can go to Bethlehem in our imaginations and really think about the miracle the shepherds saw with their own eyes.

Perhaps the greatest miracles ever is that God the Son became a man. The song reminds us that the shepherds literally beheld Him with their eyes, that Jesus appeared in the flesh. The shepherd's didn't just hear good news that night from the angels. They saw good news with their own eyes. The baby born that day was not merely a human being. He was "God of God, light of light…Word of the Father," as the song says.

QUESTIONS FOR YOUR KIDS:

1. Notice that the angels never command the shepherds to go see the baby Jesus. They just tell the shepherds what they will see if they go: a baby wrapped in swaddling cloths and lying in a manger. Why did the angels not need to tell the shepherds to go? (*Because they would naturally want to go after hearing such wonderful news. That's the way God wants our obedience to be: doing what God wants out of joy.*)

2. How do you think the shepherds felt walking to Bethlehem to see the baby? (*Probably very excited.*)

3. What does it mean to "adore" Christ, like the song says? (*It means to admire, to cherish, to delight in, to revere, to worship. When we realize who Christ is, this should be our response.*)

PRAY:

God, help us to imagine the excitement the shepherds felt that day going to Bethlehem, knowing they were going to see the King of angels. Give us the same excitement as we think about Jesus this Christmas season. Amen.

UPCYCLED RUSTIC CHRISTMAS SIGN

I grabbed this piece of wood right out of the woodpile that was destined for the fire pit, cleaned it up, and turned it into a rustic sign, welcoming the faithful to our hearth. This upcycled craft can serve as a reminder for your family through the Christmas season that we can live joyfully and triumphantly in this life because of Jesus.

SUPPLIES:

- Piece of scrap wood, any size
- Glitter
- Red, green, and black paint pens
- Pencil
- Craft glue

DIRECTIONS:

1. If you don't have any scrap wood on hand, grab an unfinished piece at a home improvement or craft store.

2. Start by writing out the lettering, drawing in the star and tree branches in pencil (if you have young kids, do this part for them). The wood is usually pretty forgiving and allows you to erase until you're happy with the design. Don't be afraid to get creative with your lettering, this is homemade after all.

3. Trace over the letters with a paint pen. You can also use paint and small brushes, but the paint pens are the easiest for lettering, especially with young children.

4. Use craft glue to outline and fill in the star at the top. Sprinkle generously with gold glitter and tap off the excess. Lay flat to dry so your glue and glitter don't run.

5. Add simple branches with green craft paint.

6. Once your sign is dry, it's ready to put in place at the front door or to rest against your fireplace. Add a hanger, and you can place it on the wall as well.

O Come, All Ye Faithful

John Francis Wade, circa 1743

♩=115

1. O come, all ye faith-ful, joy-ful and tri-um-phant, O come ye, O
2. True God of true God, Light from Light E-tern-al, Lo, He
3. Sing, choirs of an-gels, sing in ex-ul-ta-tion; O sing, all ye
4. See how the shep-herds, sum-moned to His cra-dle, Leaving their
5. Lo! star led chief-tains, Ma-gi, Christ a-dor-ing, Of - er Him
6. Child, for us sin-ners poor and in the man-ger, We would em-
7. Yea, Lord, we greet Thee, born this hap-py morn-ing; Je - sus,

come ye, to Beth-le-hem. Come and be-hold Him, born the King of an-gels;
shuns not the Vir-gin's womb; Son of the Fa-ther, be-got-ten, not creat-ed;
citi-zens of Heaven a-bove! Glor-y to God, all glor-y in the high-est;
flocks, dr-aw nigh to gaze; We too will thi-ther bend our joy-ful foot-steps;
in-ce-nse, gold, and myrrh; We to the Christ Child bring our hearts' o-bla-tions.
- brace Thee, with love and awe; Who would not love Thee, lov-ing us so dear-ly?
to Thee be all glo-ry giv'n; Word of the Fa-ther, now in flesh ap-pear-ing.

Refrain

O come, let us a-dore Him, O come, let us a-dore Him, O come, let us a-dore Him, Christ

the Lord.

STORY:

It was December 23, about 200 years ago in 1818. A group of actors were traveling in the Austrian Alps re-enacting the story of Christ's birth for different churches. Have you ever seen a Christmas play before? (*See if your child remembers one, or tell the story of one you have seen*.) These actors performed their play for a group gathered in a private home in Oberndorf.

That night, a priest named Joseph Mohr watched the play and then walked home. He reached a hilltop overlooking his village and was so struck by the quiet winter scene and the play he had just witnessed, it reminded him of a poem he wrote two years before. The next day he visited his friend, an organist named Franz Gruber, to see if he could put the poem to music so it could be sung that night at his church.

Franz reminded Father Mohr that the organ at the church was broken. They wouldn't be able to have music for the Christmas Eve service. Do you think they just gave up? (*No.*) Father Mohr went into the next room and grabbed a guitar and brought it to Franz. As Franz began to play and read the words of the poem, he said, "This song sings itself." Within a few hours, he had a tune, and the two of them presented the song that night at the Christmas Eve service. It was the first time "Silent Night" was ever performed.

The song was given to groups of traveling singers who took the song all over Europe and eventually to the United States. It was translated into English in 1863, and since then has been translated into nearly every language on earth.

SCRIPTURE: LUKE 2:16

EXPLANATION:

"Silent Night" describes the moment the shepherds left the fields to visit Jesus in the manger. The song describes a moment when they stood before the baby and all was silent. They just stood in awe thinking about the angels and staring into the face of the baby Jesus.

Imagine seeing this huge group of angels praising God, the glory of God lighting up the land, and then coming into Bethlehem to see a small, newborn baby, calmly laying in a manger. How could someone so important be so small, so helpless, so sweet? Could the Savior of the whole world really start life like all of us: as a small baby? How could God become a baby? (*See what your child thinks about this.*)

Yes, this is the amazing thing about Jesus. He was God but He was also man. He set aside all his glory and majesty and was born like any one of us. He began His life like all of us: like a small baby who needed his mom and dad to survive. This is one of the reasons He is the perfect Savior: because He completely understands what it means to be a weak human being.

QUESTIONS FOR YOUR KIDS:

1. Can you remember: after the shepherds left the fields, where did they go? (*They went to find the baby Messiah.*)

2. How could Jesus be both God and man at the same time? (*He has always existed as God. He has all the qualities of what it means to be God. He is infinite, all-knowing, all-powerful, present everywhere, and unchanging. But when Christ came to Earth to be born, set aside his majesty as God and took on all the weaknesses of a little child.*)

3. How would you act the moment you saw the baby Jesus for the first time? (*See how your child might react knowing they were looking at the holy Savior of the world.*)

PRAY:

Thank You, God, for sending Christ as a human being to Earth. He knows what it's like to be weak, so He sympathizes with us when we feel lost, alone, afraid, or tempted. Help us to trust in Him completely.

SILENT NIGHT CANDLE HOLDER

What better way to reflect on "Silent Night" than with a quiet flickering candle? A flickering flame lighting the dark night reminds us that Jesus' birth was like a candle—a light in the dark world. Make just one candle holder or enough to line your entire walkway. These also are a great way to fill the windowsills in your home. Let these candle holders remind you Jesus came as a light in the darkness.

SUPPLIES:

- Clean, dry jar
- Black craft foam
- Blue craft paint
- Black craft paint
- Craft glue
- Foam brush
- Hot glue
- Twine
- Star stickers
- Glitter
- Cotton swab

DIRECTIONS:

1. Place stickers all over jar, pressing firmly to make sure they are sticking down.

2. Paint 1-2 coats of blue paint over entire jar. Allow to dry completely (1-2 hours).

3. When the paint is dry, carefully peel the star stickers off.

4. Cut small ⅛" wide pieces of black craft foam to create a stable. Glue to the jar.

5. Use the cotton swab and the black paint to dab on simple silhouettes of Mary, Jesus, and Joseph. Practice on scrap paper first until you're happy with the results.

6. Turn the jar around and write "Silent Night" with craft glue. Practice on paper first.

7. Sprinkle glue generously with glitter, then tap the jar gently to knock off excess.

8. While the holy family and glitter are drying, carefully wrap the neck of the jar with twine and secure the end with hot glue.

9. Drop in a battery operated or a wick burning tea light inside your jar and enjoy it's pretty light. Since all the paint and art is on the outside, it is safe to use with candles.

Silent Night

Josef Mohr; trans. by Joseph F. Young

Franz Gruber (1787-1863)

1. Si - lent night, ho - ly night, All is calm, all is bright Round yon vir - gin
2. Si - lent night, ho - ly night, Shep - herds quake at the sight; Glo - ries stream from
3. Si - lent night, ho - ly night, Son of God, love's pure Light; Ra - diant beams from
4. Si - lent night, ho - ly night, Wond-rous star, lend thy light; With the an - gels

mo - ther and Child. Ho - ly In - fant, so ten-der and mild, Sleep in hea - ven-ly peace,
heav-en a - far, Heav'n-ly ho - sts sing Al-le - lu - ia! Christ the Sa - vior is born,
Thy ho - ly face With the dawn of re - de-em-ing grace, Je - sus, Lord, at Thy birth,
le - t us sing, Al - le-l - u - ia t - o our king; Christ the Sav - ior is born,

Sleep in heav-en - ly peace.
Christ the Sa - vior is born!
Je - sus, Lord, at Thy birth.
Christ the Sav - ior is born.

What Child is This?

STORY:

William Chatterton Dix was a manager of an insurance company in Glasgow, Scotland in the 1800s. At the age of 29 he was struck with a near fatal illness that left him confined to his bed for months. He suffered from a deep depression as he thought that death was coming soon. How would you feel if you thought you were dying? (*Let your child think about how scary death can be sometimes? It is okay to not like the idea of death: even those who want to go to heaven don't want to die to get there.*)

While William was sick, he called out to God. He drew close to God in his heart, and eventually God healed him of his illness. While he was sick, he spent a lot of time in prayer and reading Christian literature.

During this time of sickness he started writing hymns, poems, and carols. One of the poems he wrote was called "The Manger Throne." Later on, three verses were taken from this poem and the song "What Child is This?" was written.

SCRIPTURE: LUKE 2:17-19

EXPLANATION:

After the shepherds arrived at the stable, they told Mary and Joseph about the vision of angels they had seen out in the field. They told them what the first angel had said, that the baby was the Messiah, the Lord, the Savior. They told them about the huge assembly of angels that praised God. They told them about the bright glory of God that surrounded them.

Picture Mary sitting with her newborn baby Jesus. Maybe she remembered back to when an angel visited *her*, telling her she would give birth to a boy who would be called Son of the Most High God, a boy who would reign over Israel and the whole world forever. Maybe Mary thought about how an angel had appeared to Joseph in a dream, saying her boy would save people from their sins. Now these shepherds were talking about not just one angel but an assembly of angels praising God for the birth of her boy.

Imagine her holding her baby looking down at his face, saying, "What child is this?" How do you think Mary felt holding her baby as she thought about what all these angels said? (*See what your child thinks about this.*)

QUESTIONS FOR YOUR KIDS:

1. Can you remember: who heard the shepherd's story when they got to the manger to see Jesus? (*Joseph and Mary*)

2. What does it mean that Mary pondered all these things in her heart? (*A lot of amazing stuff had happened to her since she got pregnant, and she didn't really understand exactly who Jesus was yet or what would happen to Him when He got older. All these visits and messages from angels gave her a lot to think about.*)

PRAY:

Thank You, God, for sending your heavenly messengers to tell us about who Jesus is. Help us to ponder in our own hearts all the amazing things Jesus has done.

MANGER AND CROSS MINI-WREATH

While Christmas is about the birth of Jesus, it also gives us a chance to reflect on his life and death. Studying the song, "What Child is This?" you'll see the stretch of Jesus' years from a babe in the manger to the man who willingly carried his own cross. This simple wreath is a way to acknowledge both his birth and death.

SUPPLIES:

- 6-8 inch Small grapevine wreath
- Regular sized craft stick
- 3 mini craft sticks
- Hay, raffia, or burlap
- Small nail
- Purple craft foam.
- Hot glue gun and glue stick or craft glue
- ½" ribbon
- Clear polyurethane spray (optional)

DIRECTIONS:

1. Create a manger by crossing two small craft sticks and securing with hot glue or craft glue. Attach a bit of straw or ragged burlap to the back with glue to create hay.

2. Make the cross by attaching a small craft stick across a standard sized craft stick with glue. Cut a 4" strip of purple craft foam to drape over the cross, attach a nail.

3. Secure your manger and cross to the wreath. Be generous with the glue so it holds tight. Spray with a coat or two of clear polyurethane spray to protect it, if you wish to hang it outside or for longevity.

4. Attach a pretty colored ribbon to add some more color and hang your wreath.

What Child Is This?

William Chatterton Dix, 1865   16th Century English Tune

1. What Child is this who, laid to rest On Ma-ry's lap is sleep-ing? Whom
2. Why lies He in such mean es-tate, Where ox and ass are feed-ing? Good
3. So bring Him in-cense, gold and myrrh, Come peas-ant, king to own Him; The

an-gels greet with an-thems sweet, While shep-herds watch are keep-ing?
Christ-ians, fear, for sin-ners here The si-lent Word is plead-ing.
King of kings sal-va-tion brings, Let lov-ing hearts en-throne Him.

This, this is Christ the King, Whom shep-herds guard and
Nails, spear shall pierce Him through, The cross be borne for
Raise, raise a song on high, The vir-gin sings her

an-gels sing; Haste, haste, to bring Him laud, The Babe, the Son of Ma-ry.
me, for you. Hail, hail the Word made flesh, The Babe, the Son of Ma-ry.
lul-la-by. Joy, joy for Christ is born, The Babe, the Son of Ma-ry.

Angels We Have Heard on High

STORY:

In the second century, only about 100 years after Jesus died, the leader of the church of Rome, Telesphorus, said that the night we celebrate Jesus' birth, churches everywhere should sing the what he called "The Angels' Hymn"—the same words the angels said the night Jesus was born. Those words began with "Glory to God in the Highest."

Later on, those words were translated into Latin: "Gloria in excelsis Deo!" Can you say that? (*Help your child to pronounce it.*) The tradition continues to today: churches everywhere at Christmas sang these words to celebrate Jesus' birth.

In medieval times, shepherds in southern France had a Christmas Eve tradition: they would shout "Gloria in excelsis Deo" to each other in the fields, reminding each other of the night that angels appeared to the shepherds in Bethlehem. Let's hear you shout that! (*Have your child pretend he/she is a shepherd and shout out the phrase.*) It was there in southern France someone wrote a carol called "Angels in Our Countryside", some time in the 1700s. It included that familiar refrain over and over: *Gloria in excelsis Deo*. Later, in 1862 James Chadwick translated it into English, becoming the carol we know as "Angels We Have Heard on High."

SCRIPTURE: LUKE 2:20

EXPLANATION:

After the shepherds left the manger, the Bible says they returned to the fields praising God because of everything they had just seen and heard. They got to hear an angel speaking to them, a huge assembly of angels praising God, and best of all, they got to see the infant face of their Savior. They were some of the first people in the world to lay their eyes on the Son of God.

Who saw and heard them as they made their way back to the fields? Was there anyone out late at night? Do you think they woke people up with their shouting? (*Have your child think about being woken up to the sound of shepherds shouting in the street.*) It was the middle of the night and the city was filled with people who were in Bethlehem for the census. Can you imagine people waking up and looking out their windows at this group of shepherds running and dancing in the streets, echoing the words of the angels, praising God for the birth of the Messiah?

This is what the song "Angels We Have Heard on High" is all about. It is a song about what the shepherds saw and heard and how they praised God with great joy after they got to see Jesus. The song calls everyone to imagine themselves coming to Bethlehem to kneel before Christ, just like the shepherds did.

QUESTIONS FOR YOUR KIDS:

1. Can you remember: what does *Gloria in excelsis Deo* mean? (*Glory to God in the highest, which means God should be praised in the highest heavens.*)

2. Why do you think the shepherds were so excited as they went back to the fields? (*They had just seen some amazing things: the announcement of the angel, the huge assembly of angels, and the infant Jesus. How could they not be excited?*)

PRAY:

Glory to you, God, in the highest heavens for sending Christ to save us. Give us the same joy the shepherds had the night Jesus was born.

CRAFT STICK ANGELS

Oftentimes, when it comes to doing crafts with kids, simpler is better, especially when you'd like to have a low-maintenance craft for your kids' friends that come to visit. This angel craft can be used as an ornament, bookmark, or for dramatic play time. Your family can choose to create just one angel, or if you're like our family, you'll enjoy creating an entire heavenly choir.

SUPPLIES:

- Large craft sticks
- White feathers
- White or yellow chenille stem
- White craft paint
- Yellow craft paint
- Paint pens or markers
- Craft glue

DIRECTIONS:

1. Paint both sides of the craft stick white, leaving a 1" to 1 ½" gap on one side.

2. Allow paint to dry completely, at least an hour.

3. Using permanent markers with a fine tip or paint markers, draw hair and facial features.

4. Cut a 1 ½" piece of chenille stem, bend it into a halo shape, and secure to the back of the angels head with glue.

5. Finally give your angel wings. Depending on the size of your craft feathers, you may wish to cut them in half. Glue the feathers to the back of the craft stick about ¾ of the way up from the bottom.

6. To turn this craft into an ornament for your Christmas tree, simply hot glue a loop of string to the back near the angels wings.

Angels We Have Heard on High

Traditional French Carol

Edward Shippen Barnes (1887-1958)

1. An - gels we have heard on high Sweet - ly sing - ing o'er the plains,
2. Shep - herds, why this ju - bi - lee? Why your joy - ous strains pro - long?
3. Come to Beth - le - hem and see Christ Whose birth the an - gels sing;
4. See Him in a man - ger laid, Whom the choirs of an - gels praise;

And the moun-tains in re - ply E - cho-ing their joy - ous strains.
What the glad - some tid - ings be Which in - spire your heaven - ly song? Glor-
Come, a - dore on bend-ed knee, Christ the Lord, the new - born King.
Mar - y, Jo - seph, lend your aid, While our hearts in love we raise.

- i - a, in ex-cel-sis De-o! Glor-

- i - a, in ex-cel-sis De - o!

STORY:

"God Rest Ye Merry, Gentlemen" was probably written in 16th century London, but we really don't know anything about who wrote it or why. Over the centuries, it became one of the best known carols in the English-speaking world. By the 1800s, some simply called it "the old Christmas carol."

It's funny how a comma can make a big difference in a sentence. The song is not "God Rest Ye (*comma*) Merry Gentlemen" as if happy men are being asked to rest. The song is "God Rest Ye Merry (*comma*) Gentlemen." What do you think the phrase "rest you merry" means? (*See if your child can guess.*) The phrase "rest you merry" is a old phrase that meant "be joyful" or "be happy." It was a common greeting, especially at parties, that meant "good luck to you" or "good day." So the title of the song means, "Gentlemen, may God give you a good and joyful day."

The song is written in a minor key, which means, despite the fact that the song is telling people to take comfort and be joyful, the feel of the song is meant to be a little dark, a reminder that Christ came to Earth on an important mission: to save us from the power of sin.

The song sings of the time when the angels came to shepherds to announce the birth of the Son of God. When the shepherds found the boy, they found Mary kneeling before her child and their hearts were filled with sudden gladness seeing the Savior. Similarly, we should be filled with gladness at Christmas as we remember why Christ came.

SCRIPTURE: 1 JOHN 3:4-8

EXPLANATION:

The apostle John's point is clear. There are two kinds of people in the world: those who make a habit of sin, and those who practice doing what is right.

The first group live as if there is no law of God. They do whatever they want. They think they are free but they aren't. Really, they are slaves to the devil. Who is the devil? (*See what your child knows about the devil.*) Ever since our first parents sinned, this evil angel, the devil, has been the ruler of this world (John 12:31; 2 Corinthians 4:4). He tempts everyone to reject God. He tempts everyone to make created things more important than the Creator.

The second group has left their life of sin. They serve a new master now: the perfect Son of God.

John says the reason why the Son of God appeared was to take away sins and to destroy the works of the devil. This is what the song, "God Rest Ye Merry, Gentlemen", says: we should remember that Christ was born "to save us all from Satan's power when we had gone astray." This is why we should be eager to give up our sins and eager to be free of the devil's power: because the Son of God thought sin was so terrible, he was willing to leave the glory of heaven to put an end to sin.

At Christmas we need to remember the Son of God came to Earth to invade the devil's territory, to call rebellious sinners to repent and turn to God, and to give us the power to say no to sin.

QUESTIONS FOR YOUR KIDS:

1. Why does John say that Jesus came? What was Jesus' mission? (*Jesus came to takeaway sins and destroy the works of the devil.*)

2. How does Jesus take away sins? (*His death on the cross forgives us of our sins. His Holy Spirit gives us power to overcome sin. His perfect life is our example of what it means to live for God.*)

3. Why is it important to remember Jesus' mission at Christmas? (*Because we aren't just celebrating the birth of anyone. We are celebrating the birth of the Son of God who came to rescue us.*)

PRAY:

Thank you, God, for Your Son who appeared to destroy the works of the devil and put an end to sin forever. As we celebrate Jesus' birth, help us to remember why Jesus came. Amen.

CARD HANGERS

One way we send "tidings of comfort and joy" at Christmastime is through cards. Our entire family looks forward to receiving cards each year from friends and family. Checking the mail is always a happy event around Christmas. This hands-on, easy, functional craft will offer your family a way to display and enjoy the cards you receive from your friends and family.

SUPPLIES:

- Wooden clothespins
- Twine
- Red craft paint
- Green craft paint
- Glue
- Push pins
- Small stickers or miniature ornaments (optional)

DIRECTIONS:

1. Paint clothespins all over with red or green craft paint. Get creative and make patterns with the tip of your school glue and shake glitter on them to add some sparkle.

2. Clip the clothespins upright to dry completely.

3. Cut a length of twine that will be used to hang your clothespins and cards. String the twine straight across an empty wall or zig zag it to create a Christmas tree shape. Secure the line with decorative push pins. ·

4. Clip decorated clothespins randomly on the string and use to hang cards that are received throughout the season.

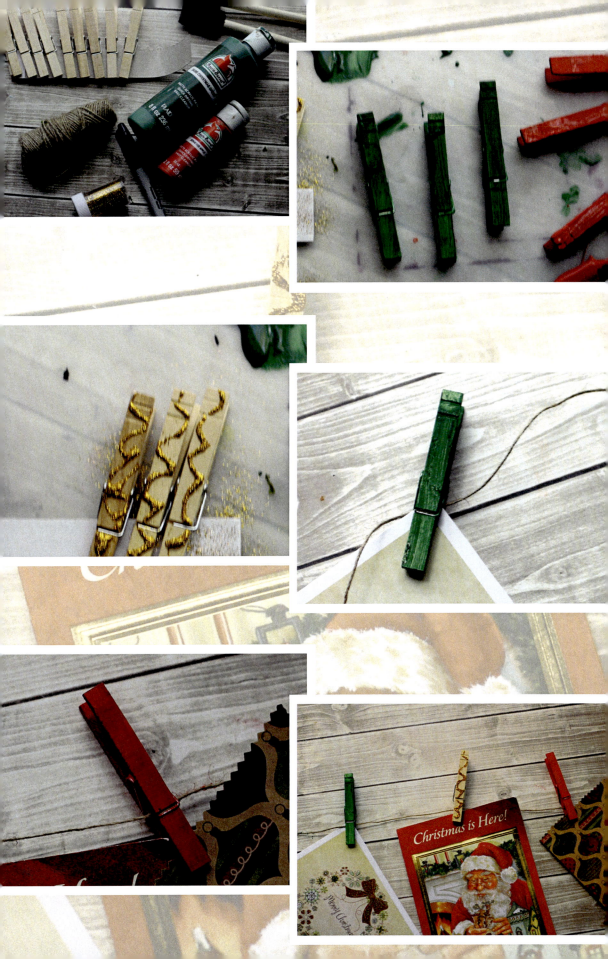

God Rest Ye Merry, Gentlemen

Traditional English Carol

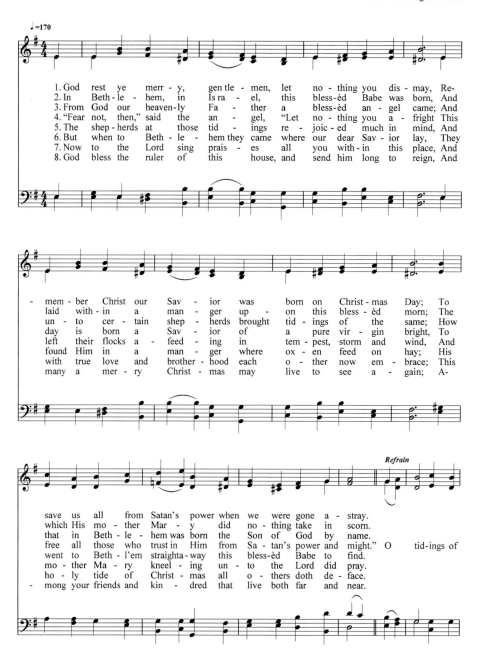

1. God rest ye merry, gentlemen, let nothing you dismay, Remember Christ our Savior was born on Christmas Day; To save us all from Satan's power when we were gone astray.
2. In Bethlehem, in Israel, this blessèd Babe was born, And laid within a manger upon this blessèd morn; The which His mother Mary did nothing take in scorn.
3. From God our heavenly Father a blessèd angel came; And unto certain shepherds brought tidings of the same; How that in Bethlehem was born the Son of God by name.
4. "Fear not, then," said the angel, "Let nothing you affright This day is born a Savior of a pure virgin bright, To free all those who trust in Him from Satan's power and might." O tidings of
5. The shepherds at those tidings rejoiced much in mind, And left their flocks a-feeding in tempest, storm and wind, And went to Beth-l'em straightaway this blessèd Babe to find.
6. But when to Bethlehem they came where our dear Savior lay, They found Him in a manger where oxen feed on hay; His mother Mary kneeling unto the Lord did pray.
7. Now to the Lord sing praises all you within this place, And with true love and brotherhood each other now embrace; This holy tide of Christmas all others doth deface.
8. God bless the ruler of this house, and send him long to reign, And many a merry Christmas may live to see again; Among your friends and kindred that live both far and near.

Refrain

The First Noel

STORY:

No one knows who wrote the song, "The First Noel", or even when it was written. It is a traditional English carol, possibly from the 15th century or even earlier, and the tune may have been brought to England from France by wandering troubadours, the traveling musicians and poets.

Noel is a French word originating from the Latin term "natalis" that means "birthday." In Early Modern English, the word became another way to say "Christmas." The song is about the very first Christmas when Jesus was born and the events that followed.

In West England the song was very popular. On Christmas Day an entire village would gather together and bring in something called a Yule log. This was a huge log that was hollowed out and filled with aromatic oils and spices. They would light the Yule log on fire as they sang this song, telling the story of Christ's birth. The hope was the Yule log would burn for 12 straight days, filling the village with a sweet smell.

After 12 days of Christmas celebration was the festival of Epiphany, which celebrates the time when wise men from the east visited Jesus. This is what most of the song, "The First Noel", is about.

SCRIPTURE: MATTHEW 2:1-7

EXPLANATION:

The wise men were probably magi who traveled from Persia or Babylon. These were men who studied the movements of the stars and planets in the sky. They traveled from East of Israel because they saw a star shining in the sky. As men who looked for signs in the stars, they were excited to travel to Israel because they believed a new king had been born there—just as the song says: "Born is the King of Israel."

When they got to Bethlehem it was well after the night Jesus was born, because by the time the wise men arrived, Jesus and his family were staying in a house in Bethlehem, no longer in the animal stable.

Even though Jesus was the king of Israel, the Messiah, the people who should have been eager to see Him—the Jewish leaders—were either not interested in seeing Him or were actually threatened by Him. King Herod the Great wanted to remain in power so he troubled to hear a new king had been born. Instead, it was people outside the nation of Israel who honored Jesus. This foreshadowed the day when the message about Jesus would go out to all the nations of the world.

QUESTIONS FOR YOUR KIDS:

1. Who were the wise men? (*Magi, meaning they were priests and astronomers from the East.*)

2. What do you think the star looked like? (*We aren't a lot about what the star looked like. It may have been very bright like the song says, but chances are it wasn't because King Herod didn't even know about the star.*)

3. Is Jesus the king of Israel only, or is He king of the whole world? (*He is both. The Scriptures promised a king would rise in Israel who would be Lord of the whole world.*)

PRAY:

Jesus, you are king of the world! Just as the Wise Men visited you long ago looking to worship you, we want to worship you, too. Make us excited to see you, just as the Magi were eager to find you long ago. Amen.

NOEL PLATE

One of my kids' favorite things to do during the holiday season is crafts. One of my favorite things to do is bake treats. This craft gives the best of both worlds. This sweet, simple craft celebrating the birth of our Savior will last for years to come. We placed the word NOEL in the center of a Christmas tree to remind my children of Christ every time they see a Christmas tree this season. There is lots of room for creativity here, so don't hold back. Encourage your children to think outside the box with their tree design.

SUPPLIES:

- Plain white plate
- Oil-based permanent markers
- Alphabet stickers

DIRECTIONS:

1. For long term use, be sure to use oil-based permanent markers. I recommend Sharpie brand, because they are non-toxic and xylene free.

2. Use alphabet stickers to spell "Noel" on the center of the plate. Press each letter firmly onto the plate, paying special attention to the edges.

3. Using a green marker, dab gently all around the letters. Make sure all the edges have paint on them so the lettering is clear and sharp.

4. Draw the rest of the tree design freehand or sketch it out with a dry erase marker first. Color it in well.

5. After the tree is completely dry, peel off the lettering. It will take approximately one hour for your paint to dry.

6. Place the plate in a *cool* oven, turn oven to 350 degrees and bake plate for 30 minutes. Let it cool inside the oven, then remove.

7. The cookie plate should be washed by hand after use.

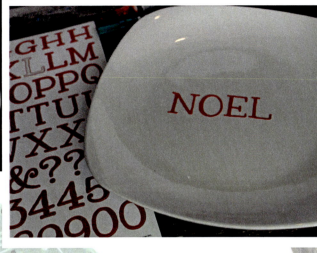

The First Noel

Traditional English Carol

We Three Kings

John Henry Hopkins, Jr. was a deacon in the Episcopal Church. He loved art and music. He worked as a church music instructor for other men who were in training to serve as ministers in their churches. He designed stained glass windows and other ornaments for church buildings. He also wrote many hymns and songs for congregations to sing. Do you know anyone who is a really good artist or musician? (*See who your child can name.*)

Hopkins went on to be a very influential rector and priest in the church. He even gave the eulogy sermon at the funeral of the American President, Ulysses S. Grant.

In 1857, his nephews and nieces were going to perform and Christmas pageant at his school, so he wrote a song to be performed at the pageant. Six years later, in the middle of America's Civil War, he published the song in his book, Carols, Hymns, and Songs. The song was called "We Three Kings."

This carol is meant to be sung by three voices, telling the story of three traveling magi coming to visit Jesus.

SCRIPTURE: MATTHEW 2:9-12

EXPLANATION:

As we said last time, the wise men were magi who traveled from the East. We don't know if there were three of them like the song says. We do know they carried three gifts with them, which is probably why people believe there might have been three wise men.

What's so shocking is how these men react to seeing this little boy. They fall down in front of Him and worship Him.

They brought gold, frankincense, and myrrh. These were very costly gifts, and they help to remind us about who Jesus really is. Who typically gets to wear things made of gold? (*Royalty.*) Gold was something kings were given; it reminds us that Jesus is a king. Frankincense was a white resin from trees that smelled good when burned, and it was used in temples when worshiping gods, so what does this gift remind us about Jesus? (*It reminds us that Jesus is God.*) Myrrh was a spice used for embalming dead bodies, so what does this gift remind us about Jesus? (*It reminds us that Jesus was a Man who would die some day for our sins.*)

QUESTIONS FOR YOUR KIDS:

1. Can you remember: how many gifts did the wise men bring? (*Three*)

2. Do you remember what the gifts were? (*Gold, frankincense, and myrrh*)

3. What do these three gifts remind us about Jesus? (*Jesus is a king. Jesus is God. Jesus died for our sins.*)

PRAY:

Thank You, God, for sending Jesus to be our king, the one we worship, and the one who was sacrificed for our sins. Give us a Christmas full of joy as we think about the greatest gift of all: Jesus Christ.

TOILET PAPER ROLL MAGI FIGURINES

Empty toilet paper rolls have long been a favorite craft item for many reasons. They are free, easily accessible, and make a wonderful blank canvas for creating just about anything you can imagine. Turn some of yours into these three magi. These are great for dramatic play, in a sensory bin, or as mantle decorations. Encourage your child to create an entire nativity scene if they enjoy crafting.

SUPPLIES:

- Empty toilet paper rolls
- Craft paint, assorted colors
- 6"x 9" craft foam, assorted
- Googly eyes
- Markers
- Glue gun/glue sticks

DIRECTIONS:

1. Make a very light line about 1 ½" to 2" from the top of your roll. Show your child how to paint the cardboard roll right up to the line, leaving the face unpainted. Allow paint to dry thoroughly.

2. To make capes for your magi, cut craft foam in half so the piece is approximately 6" x 4.5". Fold back two corners and secure with glue. Wrap the cape around the paper roll and tack in place with a generous amount of glue.

3. Add hair, beards, crowns, and gifts to carry using craft foam. Let your child explore and create by making unique characters.

4. Finally, give the magi simple faces with markers.

We Three Kings

John Henry Hopkins, Jr., 1857   John Henry Hopkins, Jr.

1. We three kings of Or-i-ent are; Bear-ing gifts we tra-verse a-
2. Born a King on Beth-le-hem's plain Gold I bring to crown Him a-
3. Frank-in-cense to of-fer have I; In-cense owns a De-i-ty
4. Myrrh is mine, its bit-ter per-fume Breathes a life of ga-ther-ing
5. Glor-ious now be-hold Him a-rise; King and God and s-ac-ri-

-far, Field and fount-ain, moor and mount-ain, Fol-low-ing yon-der
-gain, King for-ev-er, ceas-ing ne-ver, O-ver us all to
night; Prayer and prais-ing, voic-es rais-ing, Wor-ship-ping God on
gloom; Sor-rowing, sigh-ng, bleed-ing, dy-ing, Sealed in the stone cold
-fice; Al-le-lu-ia, Al-le-lu-ia, Sounds through the earth and

Refrain

star.
reign.
high.   O   star of won-der, star of light, Star with roy-al beau-ty bright,
tomb.
skies.

West-ward lead-ing, still pro-ceed-ing, Guide us to thy per-fect light.

The Holly and the Ivy

STORY:

Since ancient times, homes were decorated with holly and ivy plants in the wintertime because their leaves stayed green all winter long. In many cultures of Europe, on the longest nights of the year in late December, homes and public places were decorated with these evergreen plants to celebrate that from that point forward, there would be a little more daylight every day, eventually leading to the warmer days of spring. These plants symbolized rebirth and new life in the midst of the bitter cold of winter.

Pagan people also believed holly and ivy had magical properties to ward off evil spirits and dark powers heard in the howling winter winds. Eventually, as Christianity spread throughout Europe, these old wintertime customs remained but they were given new meaning. This is what the song, "The Holly and the Ivy", is all about. No one knows who wrote the song, but it was first published in the early 1700s using a French folk melody. It focuses on how holly plant's features remind us of Jesus.

- The holly blooms with white flowers, reminding us Jesus was born pure and free from sin.
- The holly berry is bright red like blood, reminding us Jesus died on the cross for our sins.
- The holly leaves have prickly leaves that can stab our skin, reminding us Jesus was crowned with thorns by the soldiers who crucified him.
- The bark of the holly plant has a very bitter taste, reminding us of the bitter wine Jesus was offered to drink when he was hanging on the cross.

SCRIPTURE: MARK 15:12-39

EXPLANATION:

It may seem strange to read about the day Jesus died when we are celebrating the day when Jesus was born. Why is this important? (*We should remember this is why Jesus was born into this world: so he could die for our sins.*)

When we think of the baby Jesus, we might picture a him as a cute little baby with a soft face. But we need to remember that tender face was later pierced with thorns. We might think of his small hands grasping the finger of Mary his mother. But we need to remember those hands were later pierced with nails and nailed to a splintery cross.

Crucifixion was one of the worst ways to die invented by human beings. Good citizens of the Roman Empire thought it was rude to even speak of it—something reserved only for the worst criminals. After the chief priests and leaders of the people had totally rejected Jesus, they demanded he be killed. The governor turned Jesus over to a whole battalion of soldiers—about 600 soldiers—and they mocked him. They twisted together thorns into the shape of crown and pressed it on to Jesus' head, piercing His scalp. They bowed down in front of Him, pretending to honor him like a king, while they teased Him. They punched Him, spit in His face, and hit Him with a wooden reed. Why do you think they were so cruel? (*See how your child reacts.*)

After this, Jesus was forced to carry a large beam of wood, probably weighing over 75 pounds, but He was so weakened by His beating, they had to ask another man to help Him. He walked outside the city to a place called Golgotha, which was a place they killed criminals.

They laid Him on his back, stretched out His arms, and nailed His wrists to the beam of wood using 7-inch spikes. This would have been extremely painful, sending shooting pain through His arms and back. After this they lifted the beam of wood up in the air and attached it to a long wooden post. Then they nailed His feet to the post. Jesus hung on the cross for six hours. It would have been very hard to breathe in that position. Jesus was in pain all over His body.

Why did God the Father let Jesus die this way? The Old Testament said if someone was hung on a piece of wood like this, it meant God's curse was upon him. Why would God curse His own Son? Did Jesus do something wrong? (*No. It wasn't because He had sinned. Galatians 3:13 says Jesus became a curse for us because of our sins.*)

QUESTIONS FOR YOUR KIDS:

1. What did Jesus cry out from the cross? (*My God, my God, why have you forsaken me?*)

2. Why did Jesus say this? Did God really forsake Jesus? (*At that moment, He was forsaken by His Father on the cross because He was paying for our sins. Jesus was actually quoting from Psalm 22 which prophecies about Jesus' death 1000 years before it happened.*)

3. How could Jesus pay for the sins of all His people? (*He could do this because He wasn't just a man. He was the eternal Son of God.*)

PRAY:

God, help us to remember the cross at Christmas. Help us to remember that the cross is the reason Jesus was born. Help us to remember who the baby is in the manger: the eternal Son of God who would take away the sins of the world. Amen.

HOLLY WREATH

This fun little holly wreath makes a great ornament or package decoration. In this old Christmas carol the prickly leaves of the ivy represent the crown of thorns Jesus wore when he was crucified, while the red berries are a symbol of the blood he shed. This, of course, is why Jesus came to earth: to fulfill the Scriptures through his death. Besides being a fun activity, use this little holly wreath as a reminder of the birth and ultimate sacrifice of Jesus.

SUPPLIES:

- Bowtie pasta
- Green food coloring
- Cardboard from a box (cereal, rice, pasta, etc.)
- Hand sanitizer or rubbing alcohol
- ½ inch ribbon
- Red beads
- Hot glue gun and glue sticks or craft glue

DIRECTIONS:

1. Place a generous handful of bowtie pasta in a sandwich bag, add a couple drops of green food coloring and about a ½ teaspoon of hand sanitizer or rubbing alcohol in the bag as well.

2. Close the top, shake and gently push the pasta around to distribute the color. Add more food coloring until the desired shade of green is reached.

3. Spread the colored pasta onto a paper towel and allow to dry, about 15 minutes.

4. While the pasta is drying, take a small plate or other round object and trace a circle on the plain side of your cardboard scrap. Use a smaller item like a bottle top to trace the inside of your wreath. Cut out along the lines.

5. Cover the cardboard wreath form in a thick coating of craft glue or hot glue and press the colored pasta all around. Allow to dry. Repeat on opposite side and add a double layer if desired.

6. Glue red beads randomly around the wreath. Allow the glue to dry thoroughly.

7. Add a pretty ribbon. The wreath can be hung on the tree or added to a package.

The Holly and the Ivy

Traditional

♩=113

1. The Hol-ly and the I - vy Now both are full well grown, Of all the trees that
2. The Hol-ly bears a blos-som, As white as lil - y - flower; And Ma-ry bore sweet
3. The Hol-ly bears a ber - ry, As red as an - y blood; And Ma-ry bore sweet
4. The Hol-ly bears a prick-le, As sharp as an - y thorn; And Ma-ry bore sweet
5. The Hol-ly bears a bark, As bit - ter as an - y gall; And Ma-ry bore sweet
6. The Hol-ly and the I - vy Now both are full well grown, Of all the trees that

Refrain

are in the wood, The Hol - ly bears the crown.
Je - sus Christ, To be our sweet Sav - ior.
Je - sus Christ, To do poor sin - ners good.
Je - sus Christ, On Christ-mas Day in the morn.
Je - sus Christ, For to re - deem us all.
are in the wood, The Hol - ly bears the crown.

O the ris-ing of the sun, The

run - ning of the deer, The play-ing of the mer-ry or - gan, Sweet sing-ing in the

quire, Sweet sing-ing in the quire.

Joy to the World

STORY:

Isaac Watts is remembered for many things, but one of the things he is most remembered for is writing songs. He wrote more than 750 hymns for the church in his day. How many songs do you think you know? Can you imagine writing that many songs in your life? (*See what your child thinks about this.*)

Watts loved the Psalms in the Old Testament—which were the worship songs of ancient Israel. Even though all the psalms were written before the time of Jesus, Watts wanted people to know the psalms all pointed forward to Jesus Christ.

One of the psalms Watts really loved was Psalm 98, which says, "Make a joyful noise to the Lord, all the earth...Let the rivers clap their hands; let the hills sing for joy together before the Lord, for he comes to judge the earth. He will judge the world with righteousness, and the peoples with equity" (*vv.4a, 8-9*). Ultimately, Watts knew who would be the one to come and make the world right again: Jesus Christ. Just like the psalm says, this should make us joyful! So about 300 years ago, at the age of 45, Watts wrote the hymn "Joy to the World."

"Joy to the World" is actually a song about the second time Jesus will come to earth, when He will come to change the world forever. Did you know Jesus will come to Earth not just once, but twice? (*See what your child knows about the second coming of Christ.*) Over time, people began associating the song with Christmas, the first time Jesus came to earth. The song is a great reminder that the child in the manger is no ordinary child, but the one who will come some day to judge the world.

SCRIPTURE: REVELATION 19:6-9

EXPLANATION:

The first time Jesus came, the angel's message to the shepherds was they were about to hear news of great joy and gladness. The Messiah had been born!

This passage is about the second time Jesus will come. At that time the angels and all in heaven will cry out again, and just like the first time, they will shout a message of joy, saying, "Let us rejoice and exult!"

In "Joy to the World", Isaac Watt's writes that He comes to save us from "the curse." Back at the beginning of the world, back when the first people sinned against

God, God punished us with a curse. He said that because of our sin, our lives would have pain, hard work, conflict, and eventually death. But when Jesus comes back, he will take away sin and death forever. When Jesus comes, he will take away the curse. Instead the church will be bright and pure, clothed in good deeds, and we will live with Christ forever.

That's why Jesus is called the Savior. Just like the song says, "He comes to make his blessing flow far as the curse is found."

QUESTIONS FOR YOUR KIDS:

1. In both the Christmas story and in this passage, the multitude of angels sing out a song of joy. Why are they joyful? (*Because Christ has come.*)

2. What does this passage mean that the church has made herself ready for Jesus' return? (*Just like a bride gets herself pretty for her wedding day, Christians spend their lives making themselves beautiful for Christ, filling our lives with good deeds.*)

3. As the song says, when Jesus returns, He will reign as the King of the Earth, and He will rule the world with truth and grace. Why should we remember this at Christmas? (*The Christmas story is incomplete without knowing the baby in the manger is really the King of Kings and Lord of Lords.*)

PRAY:

Thank You, God, for sending Jesus to be our perfect King and our perfect Savior. We look forward to the day when He will come back to make this world our perfect home!

JOY TO THE WORLD WINDOW CLINGS

My twins love window clings. They love decorating the windows. Sure, you can go to the store and buy window clings for the various holidays, but it is so much more fun to make your own at home. You can create more for less money and customize them with words and pictures you may never see at the store. These are one of our favorite homemade craft projects, and I think they'll be one of yours too!

SUPPLIES:

- White school glue
- Red, yellow, and green craft paint
- Plastic baggies
- Plain white paper
- Black marker

DIRECTIONS:

1. Mix half a bottle of glue with each color of craft paint and shake well to combine.

2. Use a round container and trace a circle, about 5 inches in diameter, onto a small sheet of plain white paper. Then draw rough shapes of the continents.

3. Slip the paper with the world drawing into a plastic baggie. Press the air out to seal it.

4. Trace the outline of the globe with blue paint/glue. Then trace the inside of the continents with green. Fill in the continents with green and the oceans with blue. Be sure to start in the middle and work your way out because the glue will spread.

5. Freehand or have your child trace the word "joy" with red paint/glue on another zip-lock bag.

6. Leave your window clings on a firm surface to dry for at least 24 hours.

7. Once your clings are completely dry, peel them gently off the plastic bags. Lightly mist your windows with water or clean them with window cleaner and leave the windows slightly damp prior to sticking them on the window.

Joy to the World

Isaac Watts, 1719

Lowell Mason, 1836

1. Joy to the world, the Lord is come! Let earth re - ceive her king; Let every heart pre - pare Him room, And Heav'n and na - ture sing, And Heav'n and na - ture sing, And Heaven, and Heaven, and na - ture sing.

2. Joy to the world, the Sav - ior reigns! Let men their songs em - ploy; While fields and floods, rocks, hills and plains Re - peat the sound-ing joy, Re - peat the sound-ing joy, Re - peat, re - peat, the sound-ing joy.

3. No more let sins and sor - rows grow, Nor thorns in - fest the ground; He comes to make His bless-ings flow Far as the curse is found, Far as the curse is found, Far as, far as, the curse is found.

4. He rules the world with truth and grace, And makes the na - tions prove The glo - ries of His right-eous - ness, And won - ders of His love, And won - ders of His love, And won - ders, won - ders, of His love.

Made in the USA
San Bernardino, CA
12 November 2017